Those Were the Days

THOSE WERE THE DAYS

A Nostalgic Journey
Through the Century's First Six Decades

With a Narrative by Robert Aldace Wood

♛ HALLMARK CROWN EDITIONS

This book was prepared in consultation with
Professor Stanley B. Parsons, Department of History,
University of Missouri-Kansas City.

Set in Olympus.
Printed on Hallmark Crown Royale paper.
Designed by William M. Gilmore.
Cover Design by Robert Haas.

Photographic Credits: American Stock Photos, page 60 (UL).
Brown Brothers, cover, end papers, pages 3, 16 (R). Culver Pictures, pages 5 (UR), 8, 9, 10 (LL), 11, 15, 17, 18, 19 (UL), (UR),
20 (R), 22, 24 (LL), 25, 26, 27 (UR), (L), 28, 29, 30, 31 (R), 33
(UL), 36 (R), 37, 39 (UL), (LL), (LC), (LR), 40 (L), 42, 43,
44, 45, 46, 47 (LL), (LR), 48, 49, 50, 51, 52, 53, 57, 58 (LL), 59,
62 (U). Walt Disney Productions, © Walt Disney Productions,
pages 58 (UL), 60 (LL). Richard Fanolio, title page. Movie Star
News, page 36 (UL). National Aeronautics and Space Adminis-
tration, page 62 (L). John Ripley, pages 16 (UL), (LL), 20 (UL).
Ray Stuart, pages 6, 10 (R), 23 (R), 35 (U), 36 (CL), (LL), 56 (L),
61 (R). United Press International, pages 13, 19 (UC), 24 (U),
27 (UL), 31 (UL), 38, 39 (UC), (UR), 54, 56 (UR), 60 (UR), (LR),
61 (U). Wide World Photos, pages 4, 5 (LR), 14, 19 (L), 20 (LL),
21, 23 (U), 32, 33 (LR), 34, 35 (L), 40 (UR), 41, 47 (U), 55.

Those Were the Days

LAUNCHING A NEW CENTURY 1900/1910

Those were the days — the gilded days when America enjoyed all she needed of peace, prosperity, and the five-cent cigar. America in this age of innocence was a country governed by moral absolutes. Rules were simple: nice people just didn't mention sex or cigarettes. President McKinley once shied away from a news photographer, saying, "We must not let the young men of the country see their president smoking."

Saloons of the period, however, served as exclusively masculine havens for personal indulgence. Men in cities all over the country often retreated to their favorite watering places to slake their thirsts and rekindle flagging mental energies. These "males only" refuges were symptomatic in an era of male supremacy. Women were banned by statute from voting booths, tobacco shops, and some restaurants. One audacious female was arrested in 1904 for smoking in public. *Cosmopolitan* Magazine commented in 1905: "There is something mentally enervating in feminine companionship."

New York's Fifth Avenue at the turn of the century.

Fritz' Cafe, at Dutch and Fulton Streets, New York City.

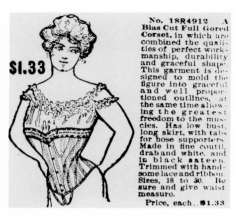

No. 18R4912 A Bias Cut Full Gored Corset, in which are combined the qualities of perfect workmanship, durability and graceful shape. This garment is designed to mold the figure into graceful and well proportioned outlines, at the same time allowing the greatest freedom to the muscles. Has low bust, long skirt, with tabs for hose supporters. Made in fine coutil, drab and white, and in black sateen. Trimmed with handsome lace and ribbon. Sizes, 18 to 30. Be sure and give waist measure.

Price, each.. $1.33

$1.33

Corset ads such as this contributed to the popularity of the wasp waist look.

Nevertheless, women were not without their God-given defenses. This was the age of the hourglass figure. The girl who was blessed with an ample bosom and who dared to show a little ankle was sure to flutter pulses. One disturbed critic accused Ziegfeld Follies star Anna Held of causing sexual unrest with her lovely legs and 18-inch waist. Anna took advantage of the free publicity and began posing for provocative underwear ads. What she had any woman could purchase through the magic of the "Anna Held Fitted Petticoat."

Women endured much in order to enhance their natural charms, particularly the coveted wasp waist. The cosmetic torture of a whalebone corset guaranteed a slim, sylphlike middle through the application of fifty pounds of pressure per square inch. This naturally resulted in poor circulation and a lack of air—and probably accounted for milady's habit of swooning at the drop of a hat.

The Gibson girl, the era's quintessence of feminine charm, had a fatal effect on men's hearts. Millions of dollars were spent on clothing for would-be Gibson girls ($14 million on corsets alone). Fashion's crowning glory was the plumed chapeau. The fancy for feathers of ostrich, purple grackles, skylarks and other birds contributed to a prodigious slaughter, and at the height of the craze a London auction disposed of the feathers of 24,000 egrets!

This daring lass relies upon her own charms to catch the eyes of admiring gentlemen.

THE GIBSON GIRL

Although only a pen-and-ink spoof of society, Charles Gibson's creation was taken seriously by admiring swains who pinned her picture to bedroom walls. Glamour-anxious girls imitated her upswept hair and taffeta-ruffled gowns.

*Christy Mathewson and Ty Cobb wowed the fans and won a loyal
following during the early part of the century. When baseball cards
were invented, Mathewson, Cobb and other stars also became the
principals in some of baseball's most active trades.*

Momentary tragedy clouded the American scene in 1901 when anarchist Leon Czolgosz shot President McKinley twice with a .32 caliber nickel-plated Iver Johnson revolver. McKinley's death was mourned widely, and there was some apprehension about Teddy Roosevelt's assuming the presidency. But Roosevelt soon rekindled the enthusiasm and spirit of the American people. It seemed that he bounded into office baring his teeth and shouting "Bully!" With enormous zest he matched holds with judo experts, exhausted visiting dignitaries with high-level walk-a-thons, and appointed his own "tennis cabinet."

Roosevelt's love of sports was taken to heart by the American public. Boys pored over health magazines and athletic dime novels. Everyone followed the exploits of baseball's heroes. Fans sang the praises of Christy Mathewson, who won a phenomenal 37 games for the New York Giants; of Honus Wagner, the "Flying Dutchman" of the Pittsburgh Pirates; and of Detroit's legendary Ty Cobb.

Aside from the giants of the baseball diamond, there were few professional personalities who excited public interest — no movie stars as yet. Instead people searched the lives of the very rich for the kind of vicarious glamour they craved. Wealthy James Stillman achieved the ultimate in indoor plumbing when he installed a waterfall in his dining room. Rudolf Guggenheimer stocked the Waldorf's Myrtle Room with nightingales borrowed from the zoo. Not to be outdone, the Cornelius Vanderbilts imported the first act of a Broadway musical for a modest reception at their home in Newport.

The FORD
1903

The Pierce Arrow

LUXURY in a car is as much a matter of engine building as it is of upholstery. Luxury as expressed in a Pierce-Arrow means efficiency first, attractive design second, a perfectly appointed car, built around a thoroughly tried-out machine.

THE PIERCE-ARROW MOTOR CAR COMPANY, BUFFALO, N. Y.
Licensed under Selden Patent

9

Boasting and blustering are as objectionable
among nations as among individuals....
There is a homely old adage which runs:
"Speak softly and carry a big stick;
you will go far."

Theodore Roosevelt

A political cartoon
from Harper's Magazine, 1901.

BIG STICK

THE
AMERICAN
DINNER
PAIL

10

Orville Wright at the controls of his "whopper flying machine."

The favorite plaything of the affluent society was the automobile. Ads for Pierce Arrow, Oldsmobile, and the Baker Electric were clearly appeals to the status conscious. Not everyone was impressed. In 1902 the state of Vermont required that every automobile be preceded by a mature individual waving a red flag. Motorists in Tennessee were asked to post a week's notice before they could legally start on a trip. While in New York cars had to keep out of Central Park, carry a gong, and cruise no faster than nine miles an hour.

Perhaps the grandest invention of the era was what the Wright brothers nicknamed the "whopper flying machine." Yet it was not thought to be so grand at the time. When Wilbur Wright first flew a full 852 feet, the New York *Tribune* relegated this scientific breakthrough to a short squib on the sports page—underneath an account of a sand-lot football game in Brooklyn.

Airplanes acquired respectability in the waning days of the decade. Small towns remained true to the homely virtues taught by McGuffey's *Readers* and "that old-time religion." Lovers listened to the new Victor Talking Machine and necked in the nickelodeon theaters. Youngsters were thrilled by the new game of Ping-Pong. And people sang "In the Good Old Summer Time"—a song that captured the snug and easygoing pleasures of this first decade.

Freedom Now 1910/1920

Only yesterday the typical American woman was content to spend her life at home—cleaning, cooking, and caring for the children. In the second decade of the century, it seemed that she started paying greater heed to some of the nation's women's liberation movements. She began looking for adventure at any cost.

The cinematic adventure serial *The Perils of Pauline,* with its heroine Pauline Marvin, typified the new spirit of freedom among women. Pauline captured the minds of feminine America and inspired a bevy of imitations like *The Hazards of Helen* and *The Fates and Flora Fourflush.* Yesterday's woman, trussed up in suffocating corsets and social restrictions, would never have tempted

These slim, silky fashions for summer 1919 characterized the New Woman who emerged during the decade 1910-1920. It was a long way, Baby, from the old image of homebound womanhood.

13

what one magazine called "the desires that ought not to be wakened." Pauline made sure they never slept. The teaser for her ninth episode summarized:

Pauline flees to shore...persuades a hydroplane pilot to take her to safety. As they soar aloft, he lights a cigarette, flicks away the match, which lights on one of the wings, and in a few minutes the machine is in flames. Coward that he is, he grabs the only parachute and leaves her to her fate....

Farfetched? Consider the real life adventure of Texas schoolteacher Anna Edna Taylor who went over Niagara Falls in a barrel.

More pedestrian, but more significant than Anna's plunge down Niagara, was the nation's first suffragette parade—staged on New York's Fifth Avenue, May 21, 1910. It fizzled in the rain, with dozens of fair weather friends of the movement deserting the ranks. The next year the march was forty minutes late. Sidewalk sages smiled and wagged their heads, saying, "Everybody knows women are never on time." The ladies did not give up. Year after year they marched to tunes like "O, You Beautiful Doll," and "What Have I Got to Do to Make You Love Me?" By the end of the decade, the rest of America joined in on the chorus. On June 4, 1919, women were given the right to vote.

New York Suffragettes on parade.

Trench-coated and always ready for action, actress Pearl White played the title role in the Perils of Pauline *serial.*

These magic-lantern nickelodeon slides captured the excitement (as well as the problems) of motoring. Despite some tribulations, families all over America enjoyed the new experiences afforded by the Tin Lizzie.

IN MY MERRY OLDSMOBILE (1)

Come away with me, Lucille— In my merry Oldsmobile, Down the road of life we'll fly Automobubbling, you and I.

America was singing elsewhere, too—around the old piano, in music halls, and in nickelodeon theaters. This was the heyday of the "song illustrator," who led audiences in song between reels of the latest thrill-a-minute movie. With the aid of twelve or sixteen hand-colored, glass photo slides, the illustrator presented a "show and sing" theater interlude.

A favorite song theme concerned the difficulty of romance in the rumble seat, although motorists' misfortunes were not confined to spooning in the Tin Lizzie. Afraid that automobiles would frighten hens from laying, farmers harassed drivers with guerrilla tactics and legal skulduggery. It was commonly believed that farmers scrupulously maintained potholes to trap unwary drivers. One New England town reportedly posted its borders with signs saying:

**THE SPEED LIMIT THIS YEAR IS SECRET
VIOLATORS WILL BE FINED $10**

One-half Ton Lighter
Than the Big Heavy Electrics
<u>Not</u> a Small Car

The New Light Baker Electric Coupe is a full-sized light weight car of the highest possible quality. It offers all the advantages of light weight (easy steering, easy handling, low upkeep expense), **Plus** <u>Full</u> <u>Speed</u>, <u>Full</u> <u>Mileage</u>, <u>Full</u> <u>Power</u> and <u>Full</u> <u>Strength</u>.

The Baker Motor Vehicle Company
Cleveland

Broughams, Coupes, Roadsters,
Commercial Trucks

Baker
Electrics
QUALITY SERVICE

Fanny Brice

Ed Wynn

Florenz Ziegfeld delighted audiences with his Follies, whose stage settings fell between the bizarre and the hilarious....
....Still, some people preferred the circus.

Lines like that would have knocked them dead on the vaudeville stage. Vaudeville! Florenz Ziegfeld overwhelmed America with the extravagance of his Follies. Headliners Ed Wynn, W. C. Fields, Gallagher and Shean, and Fanny Brice titillated audiences from the Lodge Hall in Peoria to the glittering Palace Theater in New York.

If the people couldn't come to the theater, the theater went to them. Circuses delighted youngsters with fire-eaters and acrobats, elephants and freaks. The Chautauqua tent shows offered a more uplifting program featuring orators and evangelists. Among the latter, one of the most famous was Harry "Gatling Gun" Fogleman, who preached positive thinking at 300 words a minute.

Back at the old nickelodeon, delighted fans were gripped by the melodrama of William S. Hart and Lillian Gish. Movies were by now becoming a lucrative business. Little Mary Pickford, filmdom's ever-lovely ingenue, parlayed her dimples and ringlets into a cool $10,000 a week. Charlie Chaplin made seven times more than the president — but then, Chaplin was funnier. From their yeasty beginnings (one newsreel faked an erupting volcano with a warm keg of beer), movies were maturing into a fashionable art form typified by D. W. Griffith's epochal *The Birth of a Nation*.

William S. Hart   Mary Pickford   Charlie Chaplin

STAND BY THE
PRESIDENT

In wartime, home-front Americans
supported President Woodrow Wilson.
On the battlefront they rallied behind
the leadership of such men as Captain
Eddie Rickenbacker.

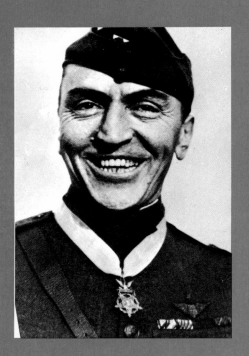

I WANT YOU
FOR U.S. ARMY
NEAREST RECRUITING STATION

James Montgomery Flagg's famous poster stirred the country's patriotism,
and thousands of boys enlisted to fight "The War to End All Wars."

Yanks from the First Regiment of the American Expeditionary Force land in France, 1917.

So strong was the Hollywood influence that when America went to war, she seemed to be following a movie script. Newspaper headlines sounded like movie marquees. In Iowa the Cedar Rapids *Gazette* shouted:

BLOOD MAD MONARCHS PREPARE DREAD SACRIFICE
FIFTEEN MILLIONS FACING DEATH
ROYALTY FORCES WRECK AND RUIN ON FATED LANDS
STUBBORN RULERS PLAY SUBJECTS AS PAWNS!

Marching into the epic "War to End All Wars," Americans sang — just as they had sung on Fifth Avenue and in the nickelodeons. Some sang that it was a long way to Berlin, "but we'll get there, Uncle Sam will find a way." Some asked, "How You Gonna Keep 'em Down on the Farm, After They've Seen Paree?" Nearly everyone sang the battle cry, "Over There!"

After American doughboys joined the war, one German officer remarked, "The attack of the American troops, with the impetuosity which the German Staff had not believed possible, brought about the ruin of the German army." For brash flamboyance the Yanks were unmatched. There was the individual brilliance of men like Eddie Rickenbacker and Sergeant Alvin York. There was also the courage and the *esprit de corps* of American Marines, who, charging in ragtag waves, skipping from rock to boulder like their Indian-fighting forebears, made a legend of Belleau Wood. Throughout the hot, fierce months of war, American units earned battle scars in similar actions.

Finally it was over. The boys came home to a country tired of scrimping, tired of fighting that bloody war. The world had been made "safe for democracy," and America was ready to let down her hair and celebrate.

21

A whispered "Joe sent me" might have opened the door to this downstairs brownstone speakeasy, one of nearly 32,000 illegal clubs operating in New York during Prohibition.

TEN YEARS OF RAZZMATAZZ 1920/1930

No sooner had Congress passed Prohibition than "Pop!" went the bootlegged champagne and a whole new era bubbled forth peopled by giddy pleasure-seekers and circus personalities. One movie marquee advertised "brilliant men, beautiful jazz babies, champagne baths, midnight revels, petting parties in the purple dawn, all ending in one terrific climax that makes you gasp." It summarized the popular conception of the era.

The man who presided over much of this heady decade was a homespun puritan named John Calvin Coolidge. Coolidge provided stability in an age when everything seemed to be running toward hell and hedonism.

Some were alarmed at the direction fashion had taken, protesting that "The low-cut gowns, the rolled hose and short skirts are born of the Devil!" And young debaters of Queens College blithely argued, "Resolved: it is easier to make love in a Ford than in a buggy."

"Silent" Cal Coolidge. A young socialite once told him she had bet a fortune on making him say at least three words. He replied tersely, "You lose."

23

These happy flappers dance through dinner in hopes of winning a Charleston endurance contest.

During the Twenties singer Rudy Vallee "vo-do-deo-doed" his way into the hearts of the nation's females. Among his biggest hits were "Vagabond Lover," "Betty Coed" and "The Whiffenpoof Song."

The life of the college campus added zest to the Twenties. White Rock and whiskey in hip flasks was as common at frat parties as cigarettes. Oh, yes—cigarette smoking doubled during the decade. And language! Out of the collegiate cult of frantic pleasure-seeking came a whole new lexicon: "Drugstore cowboys" and "cake-eaters" "carried a torch" for "ritzy shebas" radiating sex appeal. "Hep hoofers" and "gold diggers" preyed upon "spifflicated pushovers" at the local "gin mill." Was it a good time? You bet! It was "hotsy-totsy." Why, it was positively "copacetic"!

Fashion could serve as a barometer of these good times. In 1919 the average hemline hung but six inches above the ground. By the end of the decade it had cleared the knee. In those ten years America was introduced to radio broadcasting, crossword puzzles, bathing beauty contests, brokers' loan statistics, confession magazines, traffic lights, Al Capone, and other "firsts" for Jazz Age culture. Who would have believed, a generation ago, that the fashionable male of this decade would wear bell-bottom pants, raccoon coat, and a gray

"Held's Hellions," drawn by John Held Jr., caricatured the uninhibited youth cult of the Jazz Age.

Philadelphia's Public Safety Director "Duckboards" Butler smashes a keg of illegal whiskey after a raid in 1924.

fedora slung rakishly over one eye. Who would have believed that this young man and his flapper —sporting flimsy shimmy, turned down hose, cloche hat and bobbed hair—would idolize the likes of Al Capone.

Tabloids loved Al Capone, and a story like "Capone Gains Eleven Pounds" made headlines. Certainly he was a great "swell." With pistols bulging under each arm, Capone would loll royally in his armored seven-ton custom-made automobile. As pasha of the Chicago underworld, he enjoyed imported silks and flashed a $50,000 diamond ring. Like a renegade Santa Claus, Capone scattered largesse wherever he went. He shot craps for thousands of dollars a throw, but he never put any money in stocks, swearing that "Wall Street is crooked."

Prohibition cut down the total consumption of spirits in the Twenties, but disregard for the law was widespread. A common method of making illegal hooch was the condensation of industrial alcohol. A palatable whiskey substitute was then counterfeited with the aid of caramel, charred wood or even fusel oil. Unthinkingly the federal government aided the bootleg game by publishing bulletins on how to make alcohol from apples, oats and even parsnips.

"Scarface" Al Capone, the gangland leader who made a fortune bootlegging liquor to speakeasies like the one below.

Billy Sunday preached an enthusiastic moralism during the Twenties.

Clarence Darrow at the Scopes Trial. Scopes is the white-shirted young man with folded arms sitting behind Darrow.

Paradoxically the lax morals of the time did not deter a persistent and growing strain of Sunday school moralism. The strength of this rear guard fundamentalism was tested in the Tennessee heat of July 1925. John T. Scopes was brought to trial for teaching the theory of evolution, a doctrine the prosecution asserted was "undermining the faith of Tennessee's children and robbing them of their chance of eternal life." No less a man than William Jennings Bryan, three times presidential candidate, chose to press the point. He was opposed by formidable Clarence Darrow for the defense, come all the way from New York to Tennessee in his lavender suspenders.

Outside the courtroom, herds of farmers and their mules milled among the hawkers of hot dogs and lemonade. Inside, Darrow unrelentingly cross-examined Bryan "to show up fundamentalism... to prevent bigots and ignoramuses from controlling the educational system of the United States." Although Scopes was found guilty, later to escape on a technicality, it was fundamentalism that suffered humiliation and discredit.

When people weren't preoccupied with the "Monkey Trial," they were swapping gossip about flagpole sitters, sports heroes and movie stars. Sex symbol Rudolph Valentino set hearts ablaze with his sultry, bedroom eyes. His unexpected death in 1926 touched off a near-national disaster — weeping women choked eight blocks of Broadway outside the funeral home where his body lay in state, resulting in almost one hundred casualties.

Elsewhere inconsolable fans killed themselves. One suicide note explained, "It is heartbreaking to live in the past when the future is hopeless. Please look after Rudolph's pictures."

In *Son of the Sheik* Vilma Banky succumbs to Rudolph Valentino's usual style—lowered eyelids, dilated nostrils and lots of heavy breathing.

This recording hit the market soon after Valentino's death. Wailing fans made it a hit in tribute to him.

Regal

REG. U. S. PAT. OFF.

Tenor Solo.
Orchestra Acc.

6708 E

THERE'S A NEW STAR IN HEAVEN
TONIGHT—RUDOLPH VALENTINO
(J. Keirn Brennan-Jimmy McHugh-Irving Mills)
VERNON DALHART
8119-A

Life

JUNE 23, 1927

PRICE 15 CENTS

JAMES MONTGOMERY FLAGG.

EVERYBODY'S BOY!

The Baltimore Sun *said of Charles Lindbergh:* "He has exalted the race of men." *Thousands of Americans demanded that Lindbergh be accorded one of the nation's highest honors—income tax exemption. His airplane, the "Spirit of St. Louis" was placed in the Smithsonian Institution.*

30

At the start of the Wall Street crash the ticker tape could not keep pace with frantic trading. When the bottom finally dropped, Variety *told the story as well as anyone.*

In the sports world Knute Rockne was coaching the Four Horsemen of Notre Dame, Babe Ruth was clouting home runs at a torrid pace, and Man O'War was making turf history. Perhaps the greatest hero of the decade, however, was the Lone Eagle. When Charles Lindbergh completed the first nonstop solo transatlantic flight in 1927, he was greeted with tons of ticker tape. The exploits of the slender aviator were among the last golden moments in this decade.

Abruptly on October 29, 1929, the Roaring Twenties came to a premature end. The stock market crashed, dropping the average for the twenty-five leading industrials by more than half. Billions of dollars worth of profits were wiped out. Day by day the newspapers printed grim reports of disasters, while the country slipped into an economic and psychological depression. It had been a good time, but the party was finally over.

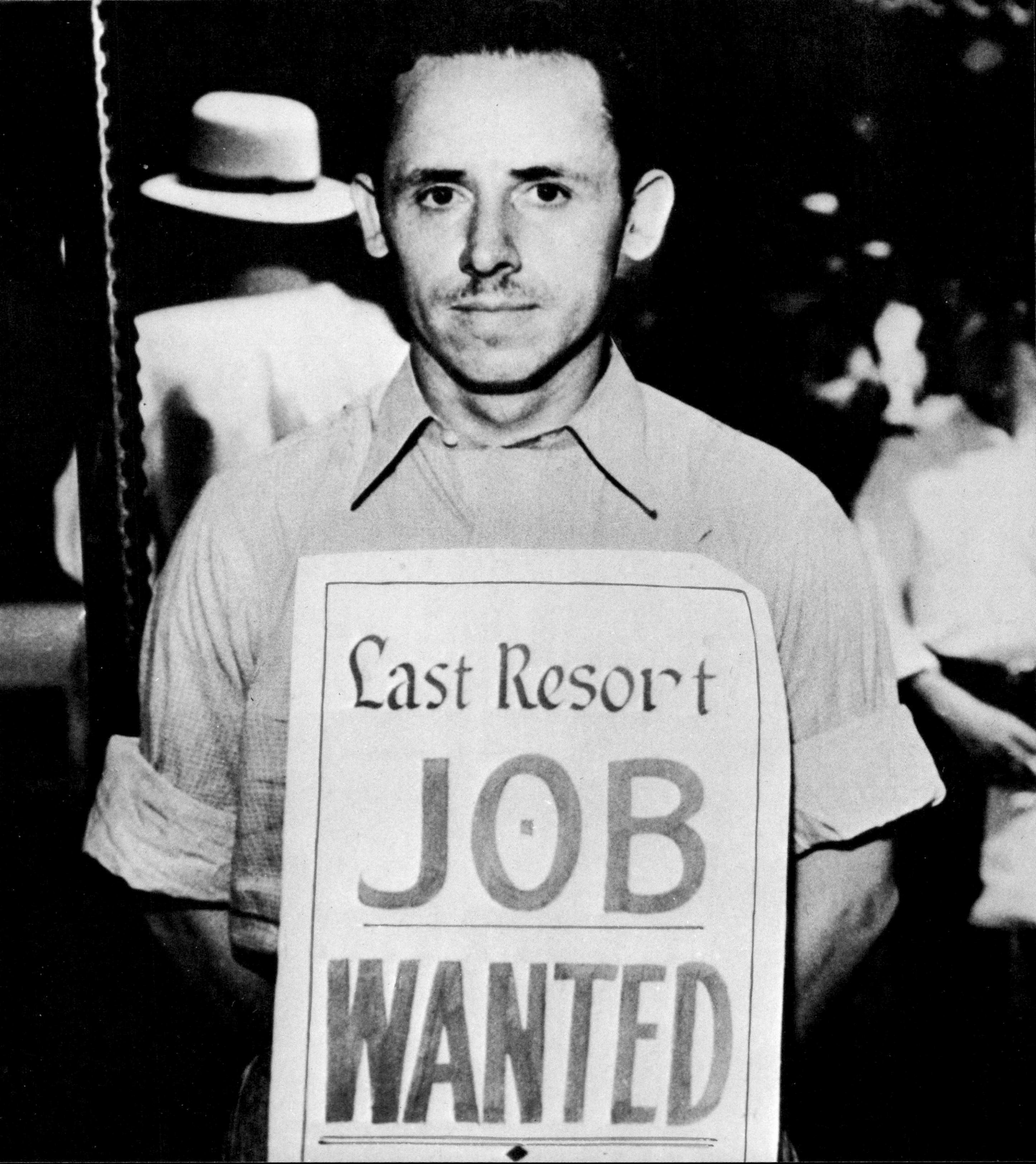
Last Resort
JOB
WANTED

"Brother, Can You Spare a Dime?" 1930/1940

Depression did not discriminate. It wrung the economic life out of everyone—young, old, wealthy or already poor. By 1932 thirteen million people were jobless. Wages dropped sixty percent from the 1929 level. "And then," as one woman phrased it, "the Lord taken a hand." As if in punishment for some unnamed offense, the great black blizzard of November 11, 1933, roared across the Midwest like a Biblical holocaust. It was a dust storm—only the first of such storms that in the next two years would lay waste to thousands of square miles of land.

Out of this dust bowl came the homeless and disheartened, three million of them uprooted by wind and hard times and left to wander across America in search of something better. Many caravanned westward following rumors of jobs in California. Some found jobs—most did not.

Hard times? No, desperate times. And Americans responded with a desperate and ingenious courage. Nebraska farmers rallied round a neighbor's homestead when it went up for bank auction. Often they literally "muscled out" the money men from the city and bought back the farm for as little as fifteen cents. Then they returned the farm to its original owner. Such altruism was not limited to rural areas. In New York eviction teams sometimes met the entire male population of an apartment building standing shoulder to shoulder in the doorway. Landlords found it difficult, if not unhealthy, to serve eviction notices under those conditions.

With their worldly possessions stowed beside their year-old daughter in a baby carriage, this couple trudged from Texas to California in the early Thirties looking for a job. There was none to be had.

33

Bonnie and Clyde strike a picture-book pose.

It was a bum rap, people said — the country was taking a beating it did not deserve. As a result the heroes of the day were those men and women who seemed to have beaten the rap. Outlaws "Legs" Diamond, Dutch Schultz and "Baby Face" Nelson won a worshipful following. Bonnie and Clyde teased police by composing verses about their crimes and sending the poems to newspapers. The poor man's best friend was "Pretty Boy" Floyd, who, so the story goes, struck back at the times by sending Christmas dinners to families on relief. Meanwhile he robbed so many Oklahoma banks that the state insurance rates doubled.

But for sheer imagination and sideshow style, America's all-star desperado was John Dillinger. Once he rolled into Greencastle, Indiana, his gun mob disguised as an on-location movie crew — complete with actors, cameras and script for a bank robbery. His actors gave a convincing performance, gutting the town bank and exiting with the loot while an audience of star-struck, hoodwinked locals looked on.

Although gangster antics provided glamour and vicarious thrills for a downtrodden public, hope for real escape seemed to rest with Franklin Delano Roosevelt. Elected president in 1932, Roosevelt encouraged the nation with "fireside chats" via the radio, giving the people confidence in his leadership. The president and his "brain trust" of thinkers and doers offered dignity to the working-man by providing jobs through CCC, WPA, and other "alphabet soup" agencies. A grateful nation elected Franklin Roosevelt to the presidency four consecutive times.

The Depression spawned a rash of get-rich-quick schemes, and thousands of people were hooked by the lure of easy money. Why not gamble when you have nothing else to lose? Slot machines, punchboards and pinball machines invaded drugstores, hotel corridors, and back rooms.

John Dillinger, his machine gun and his pistol.

Franklin Delano Roosevelt, 32nd president of the United States of America, promised at his inauguration that "this great nation will endure as it has endured, will revive and will prosper."

Films and movie stars delighted a downtrodden public. Mysterious Greta Garbo added intrigue to dull lives.

Gone With the Wind, starring Clark Gable and Vivien Leigh, recalled a romantic era.

Busby Berkeley's elaborate choreography injected color and gaiety.

Sassy Mae West spiced the times with sex and laughter. "When a girl goes bad," she quipped, "men go right after her."

King Kong was the favorite movie monster of the decade. In this classic scene Kong fights against impossible odds atop the Empire State Building.

A cheaper method of escaping the realities of the times was to go to the movies. Audiences imagined themselves a part of the splendor surrounding the 1939 premiere of *Gone With the Wind,* and they sighed for leading man Clark Gable. They wrapped their troubles in laughter with Laurel and Hardy, W. C. Fields, Will Rogers and the Marx Brothers.

Feet tapped to the happy rhythms of Astaire and Rogers. Audiences sympathized with the plight of their favorite monster, King Kong. And housewives wondered what it was that Harlow had, while husbands appraised the obvious assets of Mae West, who in the fullness of her career carried a 36-26-36 torso on a 5' 2" frame.

While movies were mainly a weekly escape, radio and comic strips provided daily relief. Kate Smith—"The Songbird of the South"—claimed some 16 million fans. She shared the airwaves with such favorites as "Amos 'n' Andy," Fred Allen and Jack Benny. Families gathered to hear George Burns deal with the scatterbrained shenanigans of Gracie Allen, and no week was complete without "Fibber McGee and Molly."

Radio also helped to popularize the "Big Band" sound of Glenn Miller, Duke Ellington, Count Basie, Harry James, the Dorsey Brothers, and Benny Goodman. These musicians elevated "swing" music to a sophisticated art form. But it was great fun, too—in the late Thirties, young "hepcats" "kicked-out" in such swing dances as the Big Apple and the Lindy Hop. As they danced they sang songs like "Boo Hoo" and "I've Got a Pocketful of Dreams."

Music master Benny Goodman plays while appreciative fans dance in the aisles.

mos 'n' Andy"   Orson Welles   George Burns and Gracie Allen

Kate Smith   Fred Allen and Jack Benny   "Fibber McGee and Molly"

Among comic strip characters Little Orphan Annie reigned supreme. Kids also kept up with the exploits of superheroes Flash Gordon, Buck Rogers and Tarzan. And with gangsters running wild all over the countryside, Dick Tracy pinned on a badge and began his campaign to rid the world of crime.

In 1939 America indulged her fantasies in the biggest, most extravagant international exposition ever—the New York World's Fair. It was an optimistic end to a decade that began in squalor and hopelessness. Throngs of people waited hours to get into General Motors' "Futurama." What they saw there was the shape of the future—a designer's projection of what America would be like in the Sixties. As the crowds gazed in awe, they could forget where they had been. The future had opened and they were on their way.

One memorable fad of the Thirties was the marathon dance. Huge purses were paid to the winners, and couples punished themselves brutally for a chance at the money.

In addition to reading the daily newspaper, fans could keep up with their favorite comic heroes in "Big Little Books."

40

President Roosevelt pays a visit to the site of the 1939
New York World's Fair. To the crowds who later flocked to the
Fair the familiar ball and spire symbolized the shape of the
future. The Fair closed the decade on a happy note of optimism.

41

WAR AND RECUPERATION 1940/1950

The first days of 1940 grew increasingly dark. America watched and waited uneasily while war engulfed much of Europe. "This Is London," CBS's Edward R. Murrow said from atop buildings there—and you could hear the bombers overhead. Impassioned Americans began to speak in support of aid to the beleaguered democracies. Others spoke just as vehemently in favor of staying out of the war entirely. The matter was settled on the morning of December 7, 1941, with Japan's attack on Pearl Harbor. America would again have to fight to preserve her way of life.

The portents of disaster had been unmistakable. In 1940 the United States cracked "Purple," Japan's top diplomatic code. On one occasion Navy Secretary Knox sent a memo to a high government official indicating that hostilities would be initiated in an attack at the Pearl Harbor base. Since 1931 graduating classes at Japan's naval academy had faced the same exam question: "How would you carry out a surprise attack on Pearl Harbor?" Nevertheless the Pearl Fleet was caught napping. As Senator Burton K. Wheeler of Montana said, "The only thing to do now is to lick the hell out of them."

Hope for peace vanished with Japan's attack on Pearl Harbor.
In 110 minutes the Japanese destroyed or damaged eight battleships, three light cruisers, and 188 airplanes.

The war meant rationing at home with coupons necessary to buy gas, food and clothing.

LOOSE TALK CAN CAUSE THIS

In many American factories posters reminded workers that infiltration by the enemy was a very real possibility.

On the home front Americans rolled up their sleeves and pitched in to sustain the war effort. Children saved toys and toothpaste tubes for the scrap metal drive. Shovels and radiators meant rifles and bullets. In Boston a buggy, a Gatling gun, and Governor Saltonstall's private rowing machine were all tapped for a higher destiny as 20 mm shells. The Boy Scouts and other groups launched paper drives. A Seattle shoemaker contributed six tons of rubber heels to the war materials drive and Babe Ruth bought defense bonds — $50,000 at a time. Victory Gardens bloomed in such places as the Portland (Oregon) Zoo, Chicago's Cook County Jail, and in backyards everywhere.

Even Superman helped. The favorite radio and comic strip hero flunked his Army physical because his X-ray vision caused him to see *through* the eye chart and read a chart behind it. Still he served proudly, selling bonds and enlisting aid for the Red Cross.

American women made a vital contribution to the country's war strength. Over 3.5 million of them joined the work force on America's assembly lines. The women of the Red Cross helped enormously — the day after Pearl Harbor, 3,740 chapters mustered volunteers to roll bandages and aid the wounded. Millions gave blood, and women from many organizations worked ten or more hours a day. The ladies

American soldiers unload supplies at Iwo Jima.

During World War II the makers of Lucky Strike cigarettes changed the color of their package from green to white. Claiming that the green dye was needed for the war effort, Lucky's ad agency came up with a new slogan: "Lucky Strike green has gone to war."

45

Pinups of Betty Grable, "the girl with the million dollar legs," made the soldier's life a little brighter.

Aboard the battleship Missouri *General Douglas MacArthur accepts the surrender of imperial Japan. "Let us pray that peace be now restored to the world," MacArthur said, "and that God will preserve it always."*

helped in other ways, too. Pinups of such glamour girls as Betty Grable and Lana Turner stirred the fighting blood of American soldiers and reminded them of what was waiting back home. In camps all over Europe boys sang "Don't Sit Under the Apple Tree With Anyone Else But Me." In towns all over America girls waited hopefully, singing "When the Lights Go On Again."

And the lights *did* go on again — for America and her Allies. May 14, 1945, brought a victory in Europe. A few months later, with President Truman giving the orders, atomic bombs fell on Hiroshima and Nagasaki, ending the war with Japan. It had been long and hard, and when the boys came marching home they set about to make up the time they had lost.

Even Betty Grable couldn't compete with a letter from home.

Franklin Roosevelt did not live to see the end of the war—he died of a cerebral hemorrhage in April of 1945, one month before victory in Europe and four months before victory in Japan. This woman weeps as she views Roosevelt's funeral cortege. Millions shared her grief.

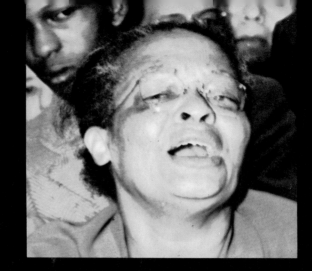

Cheering crowds mobbed Times Square to celebrate the announcement of victory in Europe.

With the war over, this sailor collects his just reward.

It was a good world in which to forget the war and all connected with it. Young people cultivated a studied sloppiness epitomized by blue jeans, the "sloppy joe" sweater and flapping shirttails. Saddle shoes, loafers and even Army boots were mixed and matched in an effort at random fashion. For dressy occasions smoothies donned zoot suits—"with a reet pleat and a drape shape." According to a Purdue University poll of the time, fully one-third of these young Americans considered *acne* to be their most serious problem.

Every day at the local malt shop kids met to feed nickles into the jukebox and dance the jitterbug. Nonsense songs like "Mairzy Doats," "Hut-Sut Rawlson" and "Chickery Chick" enjoyed much success during this decade.

Favorite crooners included Perry Como, Bing Crosby and the Mills Brothers. But of course the undisputed king of them all was a skinny, curly haired kid named Francis Albert Sinatra. One critic said that listening to Sinatra was like being stroked by a hand covered with cold cream. Criticism notwithstanding, Sinatra packed them in at the Paramount Theatre where thousands of femme-fans swooned to his vocal stroking.

Comic book favorites of the Forties ranged from the domestically befuddled Blondie to Superman.

Wherever Frankie went crowds were sure to follow. Other big names in the music and entertainment field were trumpeter and bandleader Harry James and the Andrews Sisters.

Joe DiMaggio slugged his way to fame with the New York Yankees. In 1941 the great center fielder hit safely in 56 consecutive games.

Not everyone succumbed to Sinatra-itis. Stay-at-homes read the romance *Forever Amber*. Theatergoers applauded the opening of Broadway classics like *Harvey, Life With Father* and *Arsenic and Old Lace*. It was a fine time for musicals, too, with the brilliant team of Rodgers and Hammerstein treating the world to *Oklahoma!, Carousel* and *South Pacific* in rapid succession.

In sports, boxing fans shed a tear as they watched aging champ Joe Louis lose a 15-round decision to challenger Ezzard Charles. Baseball's Joe DiMaggio kept them on their feet in Yankee Stadium and Ted Williams did the same in Boston. In 1947 the previously all-white major leagues admitted their first Negro player. Jackie Robinson was his name, and he made Rookie of the Year.

After the war many new "democratic luxuries" appeared—deep freezes, dishwashers, power lawn mowers and especially television sets. By 1949 Americans were buying 100,000 TV's a week. And *everybody* seemed to want a new car. People talked about the number of months they had "had their names in" with auto dealers. When cars came back, they were streamlined, but some—like the Hudson, the Kaiser, the Studebaker—were on the road to extinction.

Many Americans considered victory in World War II proof of the rightness of democracy. But in the four years following the war, events took place that some viewed as a threat to their way of life. The Soviet Union, disregarding its wartime agreements, established puppet governments throughout Eastern Europe. Then in the summer of 1949 came the jarring news that Russia had exploded her first atomic bomb.

Credited with initiating "the most profound change in forty years of musical comedy," *Richard Rodgers and Oscar Hammerstein scored a hit with Oklahoma. It ran for a record 2,248 performances. A later musical, South Pacific (1949), was a triumph for both the team and the musical's star, Mary Martin.*

Across Mid-Century 1950/1960

"Hey nonny ding-dong--a-lang, a-lang, a-lang!" This was the decade of Rock 'n' Roll, rebellious anthem of the Fifties — not to be understood, but to be enjoyed. "Tribal rhythms!" railed one clergyman. But Elvis Presley, king of rhythm, was not to be denied. When Elvis appeared on the Ed Sullivan show in 1956, the whole country tuned in to see this swivel-hipped phenomenon from Tupelo, Mississippi. He was literally an overnight success. And if his fans feared what effect stardom would have on him, Elvis erased their doubts: "I just want to tell ya'll not to worry," he drawled. "Them people in New York and Hollywood are not gone change me none."

Elvis did not change during the Fifties. Instead he and the rock 'n' roll cadre of Chuck Berry, Bill Haley, Buddy Holly and Little Richard changed the whole concept of pop music, driving Tony Bennett, Eddie Fisher, Rosemary Clooney, and Jo Stafford off the record charts. TV's musical program, "Your Hit Parade," was unable to cope with the new sound. "Shrimp Boats" and "Come On-a My House" were one thing, but the genteel Snooky Lansen probably felt a little uncomfortable singing "You Ain't Nothin' But a Hound Dog."

Pat Boone crooned his way onto the pop charts wearing white bucks and bearing a "boy-next-door" image.

53

First and Second Families-to-be, the Dwight Eisenhowers and the Richard Nixons celebrate their nomination at the 1952 Republican National Convention.
The presidential candidate motorcades through Wilmington, Delaware. Almost everyone seemed to like Ike.

To those who felt it and dug it, Rock 'n' Roll was a weapon of emotional release in a restless time. At the beginning of the decade, Americans found themselves fighting a war in Korea and courting the possibility of nuclear disaster. When President Truman learned of the Russian A-bomb detonation, he remarked cryptically, "That means we have no time left!"

Nationwide the reaction was just short of hysterical. In 1951 a California housewife named Ruth Calhoun broke ground for her carpeted bomb shelter, one of the first in the United States. She was scared, and enough people shared her fears to make bomb shelters a fairly lucrative business. Some wily entrepreneur even suggested marketing aluminum pajamas, lead girdles, and foil brassieres.

People suffered from atom-phobia and fantasies of visitors from strange planets. U.F.O. sightings numbered 6,000 by the end of the decade. Fearful Americans everywhere were seeing things. One man, Wisconsin's Senator Joe McCarthy, saw red.

The Communists had overrun South Korea, and in McCarthy's mind they had infiltrated the United States as well. He launched a fanatical campaign to rid America of communism. No one was exempt from suspicion. McCarthy even called President Truman and Dean Acheson "the Pied Pipers of the Politburo." Finally the Senate conducted an investigation of McCarthy's attack on the Army. The hearings were televised, and millions of Americans saw McCarthy for what he was. Once when investigators cut through his red-baiting, McCarthy conceded: "I do not have too much information...except the general statement by the agency (FBI) that there is nothing in the files to disprove his Communist connections." "McCarthyism" became a tainted word, synonymous with "character assassination." It was President Eisenhower who coined its epitaph — *"McCarthywasm."*

To many Americans Dwight Eisenhower embodied all that had made the country great. In 1952 the personable ex-World War II commander captured 33 million votes — and a landslide victory for the presidency. "I Like Ike" became more than a political slogan; it was almost a statement of national policy.

Senator Joseph McCarthy at a hearing.

If the Fifties had an adolescent hero, it was James Dean—the tousled young actor who died in the crash of his sports car in 1955. Although, as one teen-ager bemoaned, "He was dead before you knew who he was," Dean exerted a profound influence. In *Rebel Without a Cause* he stirred the souls of the young, who found some reflection of themselves in his brooding, heroic intensity. They found the same intensity and lawless energy in actor Marlon Brando and in author Jack Kerouac. Kerouac's *On the Road* was widely accepted as the "Bible of the beat generation."

A mid-Fifties teen-ager combs movie magazines for more pinups of James Dean.

Marlon Brando in a scene from the Academy Award-winning On the Waterfront.

56

In Rebel Without a Cause *James Dean* reflected the loneliness and confusion of the younger generation.

The Mouseketeers, stars of TV's "Mickey Mouse Club," entertained a generation of American youngsters. A few of the Mouseketeers, notably Annette Funicello, went on to later TV and movie fame.

A "beat" image had no place on television in this decade. Network presidents—with their fingers on the pulse of middle-class America—preferred the wholesomeness of shows like "Ozzie and Harriet," "Father Knows Best," and the irrepressible "I Love Lucy." For the kids, every afternoon was "Howdy Doody" time. TV brought America face-to-face with such radio personalities as Milton Berle, Jack Benny, "Amos 'n' Andy" and "The Lone Ranger." Another face well known to viewers was that of Jack Webb, who for seven straight years played cop Joe Friday on the "Dragnet" series.

Joe should have investigated his own industry. A rogue's gallery of television quiz shows, including "The $64,000 Question" and "Twenty-One" all proved to be rigged. With elaborate staging, contestants pretended to agonize over answers they had been fed before the show. Charles Van Doren confessed during the investigations, "I was sick at heart." Not so Teddy Nadler, biggest money winner, who bragged, "The questions they asked me hardly scratched the surface of my knowledge." Later he flunked an examination for a job as a $13-a-day census taker.

Every afternoon was "Howdy Doody" time featuring the lovable puppet and his sidekick, Buffalo Bob.

One of TV's earliest stars was Milton Berle, known during the Fifties as "Mr. Television."

The long-running "I Love Lucy" show starred Lucille Ball, Desi Arnaz, Vivian Vance and William Frawley.

Charles Van Doren ponders a question on the quiz show "Twenty-One."

The "Bop," one of the top dances of the Fifties.

Good ducktails required patience and practice.

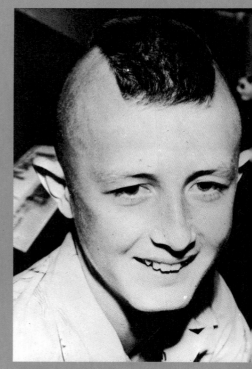

Fess Parker found fame—and fortune—as Davy Crockett.

Not everyone preferred ducktails.

The Fifties saw the rise of non-prescription cure-alls and "scientific additives" in consumer products. Some of these miracle mixtures claimed to cure anemia, diabetes, eczema and gallstones. By far the most popular additive was chlorophyll, which found its way into toothpaste, toilet tissue, salami, and even dog food.

In fashion sideburns and ducktails were "in," and the favorite colors were pink and black. Pants that buckled in the back became a social register of available males (buckle unbuckled) and boys with steady girl friends (buckle buckled). Such 3-D movies as *Bwana Devil* enjoyed a brief run, and the craze for hula hoops reached incredible proportions. Men worshipped Marilyn Monroe. Little boys worshipped Davy Crockett. In a scant seven months, record makers cut sixteen versions of "The Ballad of Davy Crockett." During the same seven months dealers sold four million coonskin caps, thereby substantially reducing the population of Australian rabbits.

Hula hoops inspired competition — with a record of over 18,000 revolutions.

Marilyn Monroe sent male temperatures soaring in this famous scene from The Seven-Year Itch.

How full, how rich were the years of this decade — and how quickly they passed! At the turn of the century it seemed that history moved at the same sputtering, hesitant pace of a Model T. In the Fifties history flew at the speed of an intercontinental ballistic missile. The decade opened with war abroad and witch hunts at home. Eisenhower ended the Korean War, and the people outgrew McCarthyism. America had safely crossed mid-century, and the future she had seen at the 1939 World's Fair was finally here. Now with a maturity born both of hard times and happy years, she was well on her way to still more exciting tomorrows.

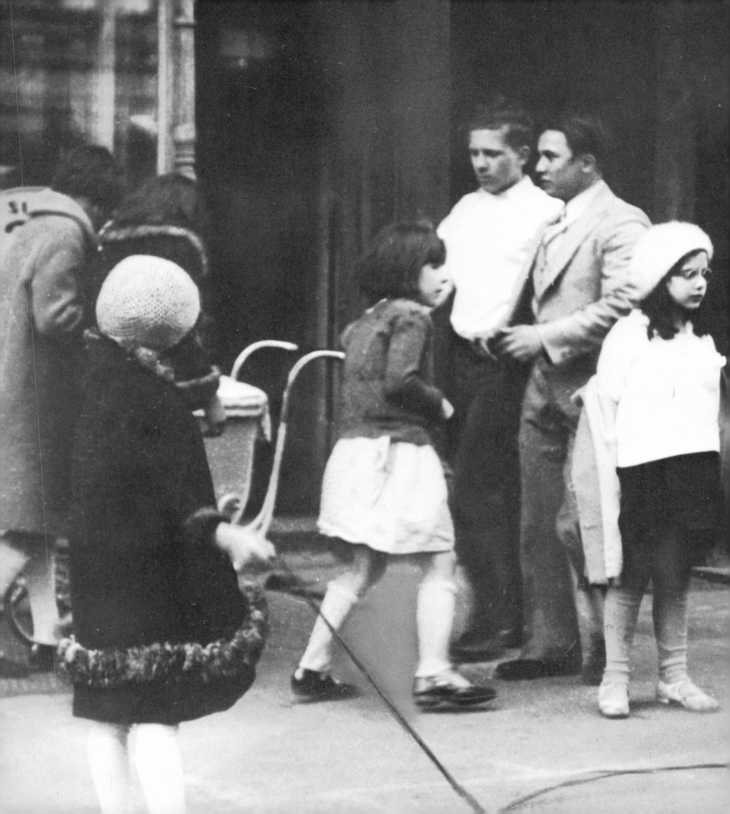